THE WOW AND THE HOW

TRANSPORTATION

CAMERON MENZIES

Gareth Stevens
PUBLISHING

Please visit our website, www.garethstevens.com. For a free color catalog of all our high-quality books, call toll free 1-800-542-2595 or fax 1-877-542-2596.

Cataloging-in-Publication Data
Names: Menzies, Cameron.
Title: Transportation / Cameron Menzies.
Description: Buffalo, NY : Gareth Stevens Publishing, 2026. | Series: The wow and the how | Includes glossary and index.
Identifiers: ISBN 9781482473186 (pbk.) | ISBN 9781482473193 (library bound) | ISBN 9781482473209 (ebook)
Subjects: LCSH: Transportation–Juvenile literature.
Classification: LCC HE152.M469 2026 | DDC 388--dc23

Published in 2026 by
Gareth Stevens Publishing
2544 Clinton St.
Buffalo, NY 14224

First published in Great Britain in 2024 by Hodder & Stoughton

Authors: Paul Rockett, Victoria Brooker, Amy Pimperton, Julia Bird, Grace Glendinning, Elise Short, Melanie Palmer

Series designer: Rocket Design (East Anglia) Ltd

Picture credits:
Alamy:PA Images 15c,15b. NASA: Johnson 10-11, KSC 11b.
Shutterstock: Aun Photographer 28b, AWKO7 4tr, Bocos Benedict 19c, Joel Calheiros 4cl, Kristina Christiakova 19b, Creative Hatti 24br, Crystal Eye Studio 7bl,Cyo bo 4-5b, 6-7, Danpastia 4tlb, 5br, Andrea Danti 4c, 24-25, Delcarmat 16-17,Deviyanthi79 9bl, Double Brain 19t, Galacticus 16c, Jason Grant fr cover c, 1c,Great_Kit 13t, Edward Haylan 13b, Oliver Hoffmann 9cl, Imaginasty 20t,Jihado Sensei 7c, Alex Kolokythas Photography 29b, Maria Korikova 24cr, Kostolom3000 3tl,17b, Magicleaf 23b, Mark_studio 18-19, Sergey Merkulov 23c,MicroOne 4cr, MrVettore 3br, 25br, Mus Illustrations 5bc,Christian Nastase fr cover tr, 1tr, Nsit 3bl, 5tr, Alena Nv 29c, 32t, Carmel Oakton 22-23, John Orsbun 2, 4tl, 26c,Patruflo 14, Psgxxx 20c, Radomir Rezny 9c, Rvector 13c, Sabelskaya 31t, Scie Pro 9cr, Shahril KHMD 12, siridhata 21b, Mariusz Szczygiel 21c, Keith Tarrier 8-9, Yana Tsap 3tr, 7br, tynyuk 5c, Rajesh Vijayakumar 28c, Vixit 26-27, Yusufdemirci 11c, Zentangle 27c, Boris Zhitkov 20b.

All additional design elements from Shutterstock or drawn by designer.

Printed in the United States of America

CPSIA compliance information: Batch #CSGS26: For further information contact Gareth Stevens at 1-800-542-2595.

CONTENTS

THE WOW OF TRANSPORTATION!

Transportation is **AMAZING!** Did you know that some trains can float, cars can be powered by poop, and submarines can stay submerged for 25 years?! WOW!

We are able to explore the world because of **HOW** we can move around. Transportation is important for helping us go to school, have fun or discover new places. We can drive, fly, float, or pedal.

Discover amazing facts about transportation, including some that may challenge what you thought you knew. Find out the science of how transportation works. Can you find some of your own **WOW** facts, too?

WOW!

Maglev trains levitate!

AMAZING TRANSPORT

Maglev trains are the fastest trains in the world!

MAGLEV TRAINS USE MAGNETS TO FLOAT OR LEVITATE 4 INCHES (10 CM) ABOVE THEIR TRACKS. THANKS TO THIS, THEY DON'T NEED WHEELS.

HOW?

Magnets have north and south poles. Put two magnets with the same poles together and they will push apart. This is what makes a maglev train levitate: The track and the belly of the train are lined with magnets with the same pole facing out. The poles repel and push the train upwards.

When different poles are close, they attract or pull together. This property is used to make the train move. The sides of the tracks are lined with alternating north and south pole magnets which pull and push the train forwards.

Maglev means:

MAGnetic **LEVitation**

WOW!

Blackbird is the fastest plane ever!

THE FASTEST SPEED EVER RECORDED FOR A MANNED AIRPLANE WAS 2,193.6 MILES (3,529.6 KM) PER HOUR. THE LOCKHEED SR-71 BLACKBIRD HAS HELD THE RECORD SINCE 1976!

HOW?

The *Blackbird*'s sharp, streamlined shape means it can cut through the air. This reduces the force of drag on the plane as it flies. The plane's light weight and powerful engines also mean it has astonishing thrust power.

It's so light because it is 92 percent titanium, which is a very hard but very light metal. Other things made of titanium can include:

Jewelry

Golf clubs

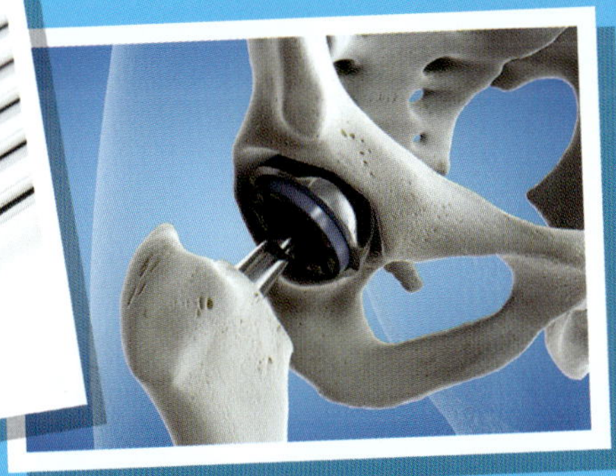

Replacement joints and teeth.

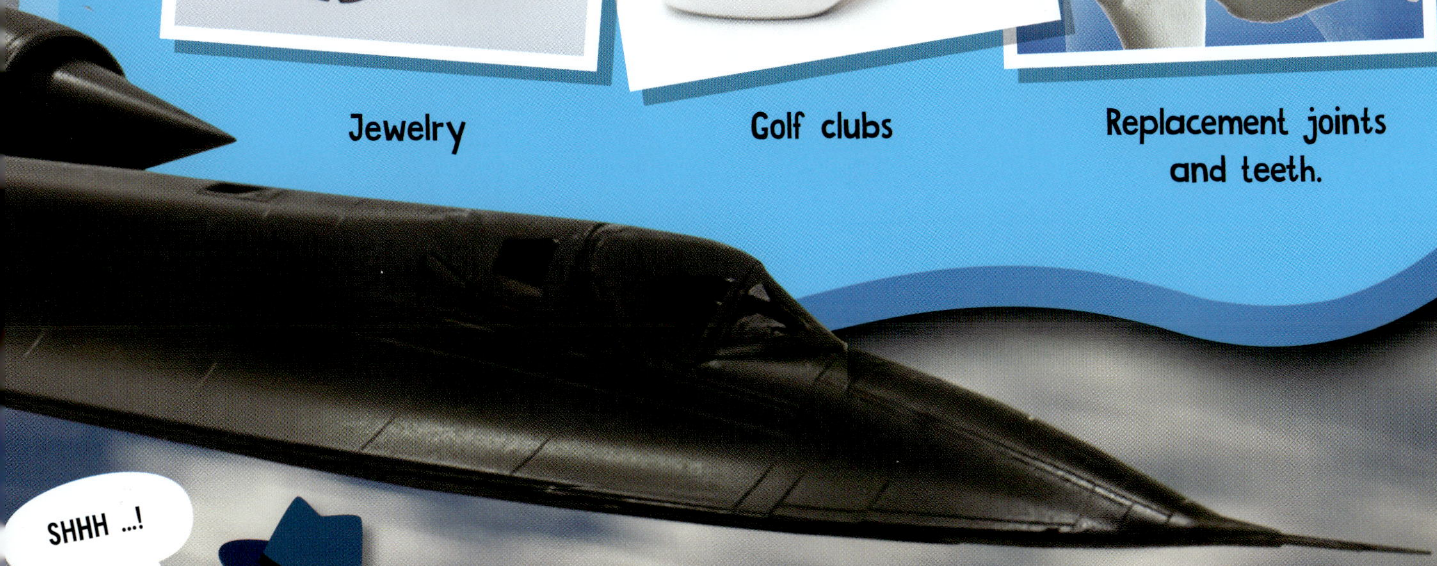

AMAZING TRANSPORT

This plane was specially designed to speed away from attack and cruise very high above the surface of Earth. It's a spy plane!

WOW!

Space rockets are so loud they could self-destruct!

NASA HAS A GENIUS WAY TO CONTROL THE SOUND:

LOTS OF WATER.

HOW?

Rocket scientists have created a system to spray thousands of gallons of water at the base of the launch pad just before take-off.

The water droplets all absorb bits of the sound waves as they are blasted out. The sound is reduced just enough to keep the rocket, and anything nearby, safe!

Four of these RS-25 engines are clustered at the bottom of some of the most powerful rockets in the world.

AMAZING TRANSPORT

Rocket engines blast into space at a speed at least 70 times faster than a race car can go!

WOW!

Hot-air balloons can't fly when it's raining!

BIG GRAY CLOUDS ON THE HORIZON MEAN HOT-AIR BALLOONS STAY ON THE GROUND. BUT WHY?

HOW?

Firstly, rain clouds are often accompanied by strong winds and storms, which can make a flight a bit bumpy (not to mention soggy).

But there's also a more scientific reason for it. Hot-air balloons work by using burners to heat the air inside them. Warm air rises in cooler air, and so hot-air balloons float up into the sky. Raindrops can cool down the top of the balloon, meaning that the pilot has to keep adding extra heat from the balloon's burners to keep the balloon airborne–or risk a quick, scary descent!

AMAZING TRANSPORT

Twice a day, every day, around 900 weather balloons are sent up into the sky around the world. They carry instruments to help to measure and predict the weather.

WOW!

A car can go faster than the speed of sound!

THRUST SSC RACED INTO THE RECORD BOOKS ON OCTOBER 15, 1997, TO BECOME THE WORLD'S FIRST SUPERSONIC CAR.

HOW?

Thrust SSC was no ordinary car. Designed to set a new World Land Speed Record, it was powered by twin Rolls Royce turbofan engines, more commonly used on fighter jets. It was driven by an RAF pilot, Andy Green, and it needed a parachute to slow it down!

Andy Green being interviewed after his epic drive

Thrust SSC's famous drive took place in the flat, scorching Black Rock Desert, in Nevada. Over a distance of 1 mile (1.6 km), *Thrust* hit speeds of 800 miles (1,228 km) per hour, beating the speed of sound by around 2 miles (3.2 km) per hour. Its phenomenal record still stands today.

BOOM!

AMAZING TRANSPORT

Thrust's speed created a thunderous **SONIC BOOM** (caused by it moving faster than the speed of sound). It was so intense that it made buildings shake over 11 miles (18 km) away.

WOW!

Dutch people cycle more than 10 billion miles a year!

THAT'S ROUGHLY THE SAME DISTANCE AS CYCLING FROM THE SUN TO NEPTUNE AND BACK–TWICE! THAT'S A LOT OF PEDAL POWER!

How?

The Netherlands has over 17 million people. About a quarter of them cycle every day. Most of the 4.8 billion bicycle journeys are short, with an average of 2 miles (3.5 km) per trip. But these all add up to a massive total yearly distance.

Bicycles work because the force used by pedaling makes the gears of a bike spin the back wheel. As the back wheel rotates, the tire uses friction to grip the ground and move the bike forwards. The front wheel keeps momentum, a force caused by movement, and is used for steering.

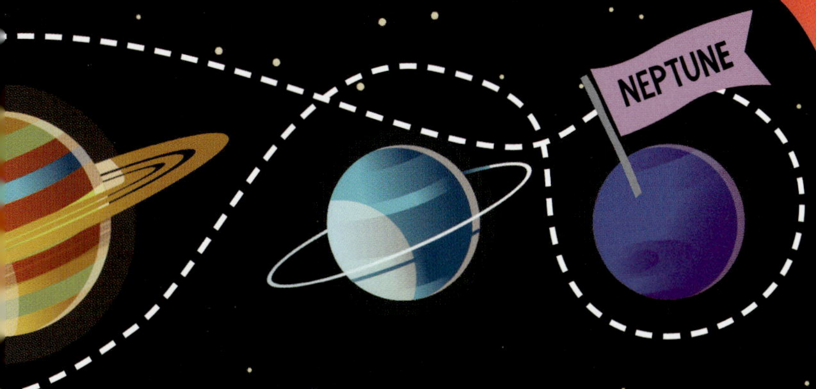

The rider is also important to keep the bike balanced. Any wobble by the rider and the bike might fall over!

Amazing Transport

There are more than a billion bicycles in the world! About half of them are in China, compared with 100 million in the United States and 22 million in the Netherlands.

WOW!

Superbikes corner inches from the ground!

THESE SUPERBIKES LEAN UP TO A STAGGERING 64 DEGREES WHEN CORNERING, WITH A RIDER'S KNEE AND ELBOW SCRAPING THE TARMAC!

HOW?

It's all about forces. As the motorbike turns a corner, centrifugal force created by the speed of the bike's wheels tries to push the bike in the opposite direction. Centrifugal means "center-fleeing." The rider leans their bike and body into the corner to balance the bike.

Speed is important too. If the motorbike leaned over that much at a slower speed, the force of gravity would be greater than the centrifugal force–and the bike would fall over.

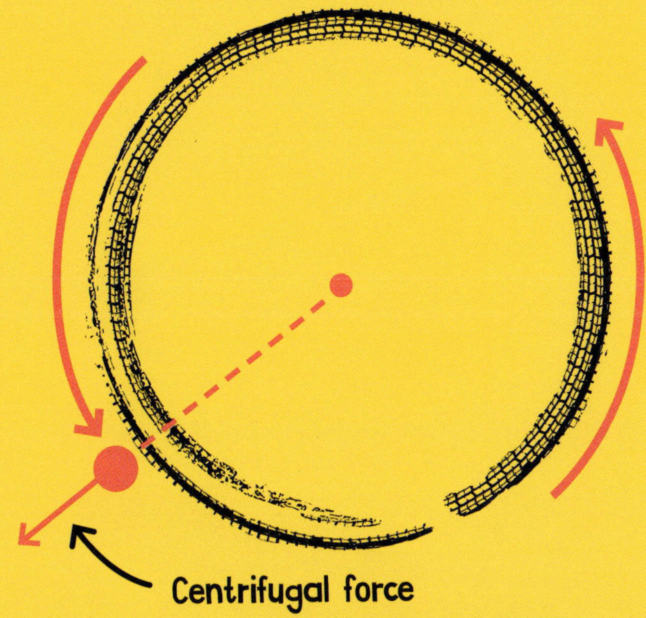

AMAZING TRANSPORT

The amount of each motorbike tire that actually touches the track as the wheels turn is the size of a credit card. That's a tiny amount of rubber responsible for gripping the track at such high speeds!

WOW!

Cars can be powered by POOP!

POOP CAN BE USED TO CREATE RENEWABLE HYDROGEN FUEL THAT POWERS CARS.

HOW?

Human waste is treated at a special sewage plant where the liquids and solids are separated. Then microorganisms are added to break down the solid sludge. This creates a biogas made up of 60 percent carbon dioxide and 40 percent methane. Carbon dioxide is removed and water vapor added. This creates hydrogen, which can be used to fuel cars.

A sewage treatment plant

AMAZING TRANSPORT

It takes more than 1,000 trips to the bathroom to power one car.

WOW!

A hovercraft can travel over land, sea, and ice!

A HOVERCRAFT FLOATS, OR HOVERS, IN THE AIR, SO IT IS PERFECT FOR CROSSING TRICKY TERRAIN OR REACHING DIFFICULT PLACES.

HOW?

A hovercraft is part plane, part boat, and part helicopter. It works by sucking in air from its large rear fans and transferring this air underneath to create an air cushion. The rubber skirt at the bottom of the hovercraft traps the air in this air cushion and enables it to hover above the ground.

The engine-powered fans also produce a motion called thrust to propel the hovercraft forward. A hovercraft can also move backward or sideways.

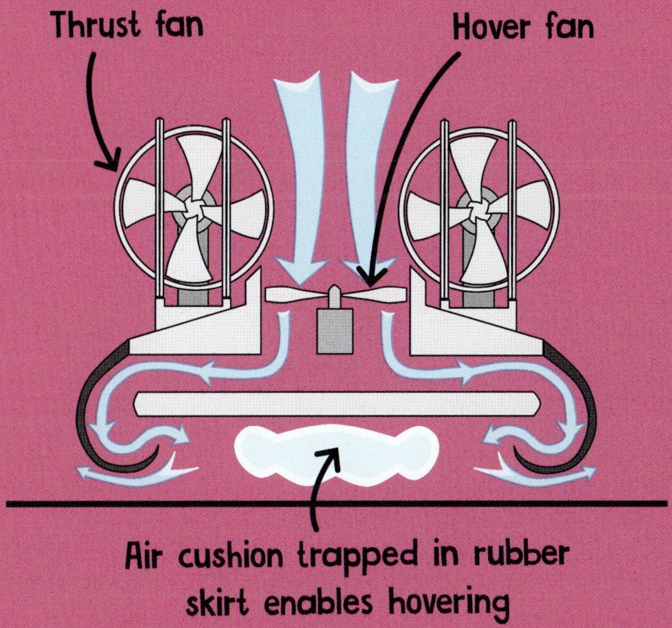

AMAZING TRANSPORT

The first design for a hovercraft included a baked beans tin and a firework! The hovercraft inventor, Christopher Cockerell, used them to prove a vehicle could float on air.

WOW!

A submarine can stay underwater for 25 years!

The only reason a submarine would need to surface is to get some more fresh food!

HOW?

What keeps a submarine underwater is weight. Submarines have huge tanks that fill with water. This water gives the submarines the weight they need to sink. When a submarine is ready to surface, it releases the water, replacing it with air, making it light enough to float to the surface.

Submarines that can stay underwater for long periods of time have been designed so that they don't need refueling. They have special machines that make oxygen from the surrounding seawater.

AMAZING TRANSPORT

HMS *Artful*, a British submarine, is 318 feet (97 m) long and weighs 8,160 tons (7,400 mt). When it enters the sea it displaces (forces out) as much water as 65 blue whales!

WOW!

A helicopter has landed on top of Mount Everest!

It's dangerous to fly around Mount Everest. That's because there are hurricane-force winds and snowstorms so flying there could cause an avalanche. But, in 2005, French pilot, Didier Delsalle, managed to land his helicopter right on top.

Helicopters can take off and land vertically, so they don't need a runway. They can also hover in the air and fly backward and sideways. A helicopter has blades, called rotors, that spin around and cause the helicopter to lift off the ground. Pilots can tilt the rotor blades, which causes the aircraft to fly in the direction the blades are tilted. In spite of 74 miles (120 km) per hour winds, the pilot showed that helicopter flights in extreme places are possible and could help to save lives in the future.

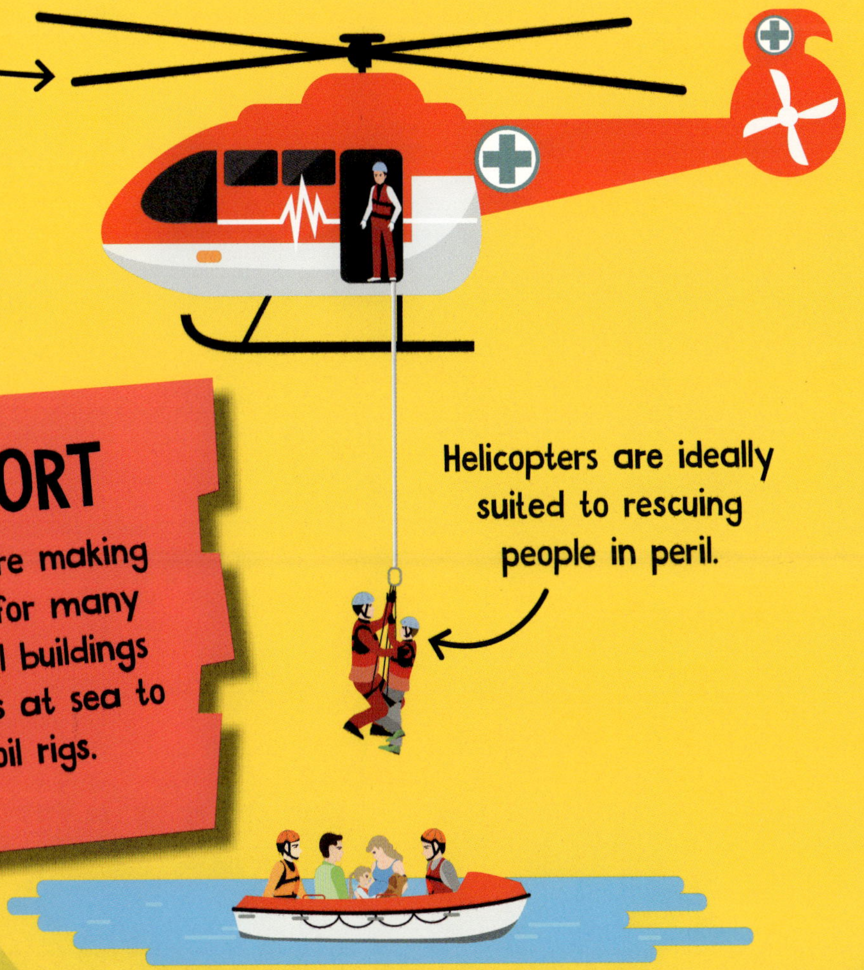

AMAZING TRANSPORT

Helicopters can fly almost anywhere making them the perfect transportation for many jobs. They can land on top of tall buildings such as hospitals, or land on ships at sea to transport crew members to oil rigs.

WOW!

Some container ships could carry a skyscraper!

Container ships are built to transport massive cargo across the oceans. A large container ship could carry something as huge as a skyscraper, such as the 108-story Willis Tower in Chicago, Illinois!

HOW?

All ships and boats partly float and partly sink. As a ship pushes into the water, the water moves away. But the water also wants to return to its original location–but as that's where the ship is now, the water pushes the ship upwards. The bigger the ship, the more water it pushes down and the more force that is pushing upwards.

A large container ship can weigh 220,000 tons (200,000 mt) and measure 1,400 feet long by 200 feet wide (425 m by 60 m). This is about the same size and weight as the Willis Tower in Chicago. Container ships are so big they could carry skyscrapers easily.

Container ships are so-called because they transport goods in containers like this. The largest ships hold an amzing 24,000 containers!

AMAZING TRANSPORT

There are millions of container ships around the world and they carry everything from cars and furniture to food and clothes.

GLOSSARY

drag the force that acts on an object moving through air or water to slow it down

friction a force between two surfaces that are trying to move, across each other, slowing them down

gears the part of a bicycle that changes the relationship between the speed of the pedals and the speed the wheels are moving

gravity the force by which all objects in the universe are attracted to each other

magnet a metal object that attracts, or pulls, some other metals towards it

microorganisms tiny living things, such as bacteria, algae, or fungi, that can only be seen using a microscope

sound wave a vibration in air or water that we hear as sound

streamlined having a smooth, even shape

thrust the force that moves an aircraft or car forwards. The force is created by the aircraft or car's engines.

Further Reading

Books

Terrific (and Trailblazing) Transportation
by Claudia Martin (Gareth Stevens Publishing, 2025)

Transportation!: Cars, Trains, Ships, & Planes as You've Never Seen Them Before
by Ian Fitzgerald, et. al (DK Publishing, 2024)

Websites

kids.britannica.com/kids/article/transportation/399628
Find out more about the history of transportation

https://science.howstuffworks.com/transport/engines-equipment/maglev-train.htm
Read about how maglev trains work here.

INDEX

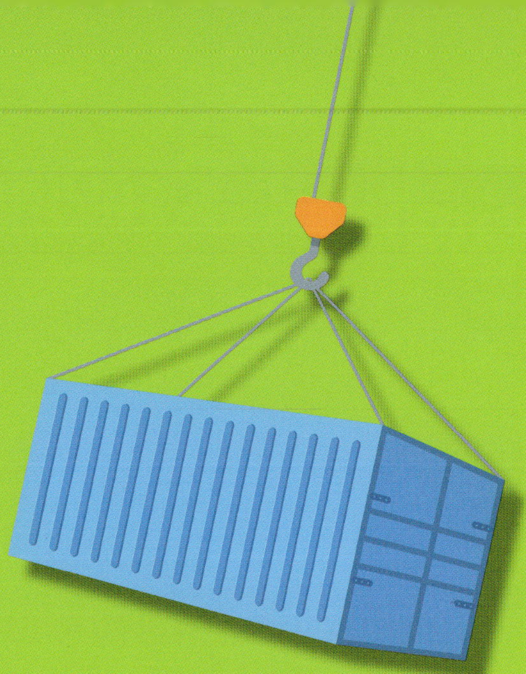